Sweetie's Healthy Start

Sweetie's Healthy Start

Terlene D. Terry-Tood

Kravitz & Sons

Kravitz and Sons LLC
204 E Arlington Blvd. Suite B
Greenville, NC 27858

Published by Kravitz and Sons LLC.

ISBN: 979-8-89639-572-0 (sc)
ISBN: 979-8-89639-573-7 (e)

*This book is dedicated to my
wonderful husband, James,
who continues to inspire and
Support me and to my greatest
cheerleader, my daughter,
Tanaya.*

Sweetie's
Healthy Start

O ur story begins in the small, quaint village of Nimativ, not too far from the Mineral Mountains. Now, Nimativ was not like any other village for miles around. Nimativ was surrounded by a beautiful, azure, crystal river that gently flowed around the village all year.

The most unusual aspect about the village was the residents. Never had one seen so many happy faces. Everyone was remarkably healthy and fit. The village people took great pride in working in their gardens and eating the most nutritious foods. Fresh vegetables and fruits were on hand in every household. Salads, whole grains, and oats were among the staples of the families of Nimativ. The purest spring drinking water was fetched from the falls of the Mineral Mountains. A variety of fresh fish was caught daily from the river by the owners of the local markets.

However, there was one exception to this scenario - the family that lived in the blue polka dot house on the back corner of Twilight Lane. No one had ever seen the occupants of the blue polka dot estate. But rumors about the family were a constant topic of hot discussion in between workouts.

Some thought the family had magical powers. Others painted pictures of "super heroes" on guard to save the village. Still others imagined the half-horse, half-man type centaur that roamed the mountains in the black of night. Whatever image was created, none could have been further from the truth. The family on Twilight Lane was very different from the other folks of Nimativ.

The name scrawled on the mailbox read "Portly." First, there was Mr. O. Bese Portly. He was short, thick, and very round and smoked the stinkiest green cigarettes, one after another. Then, there was his wife, Mrs. Patricia Plump Portly. She was at least a foot taller than her husband but was just as round. Mrs. Portly loved to eat all her food fried: fried breakfast, refried lunches, and deep fried dinners. She fried everything she put in her mouth.

Then there were the Portly children. The son, Craven, craved only processed junk food. Since it was not sold in the village, he spent hours on the Internet ordering whatever he could afford: all kinds of chips, slackpacks, crackers, and processed foods. Why, he even ordered fast food from the burger and chicken joints in other towns.

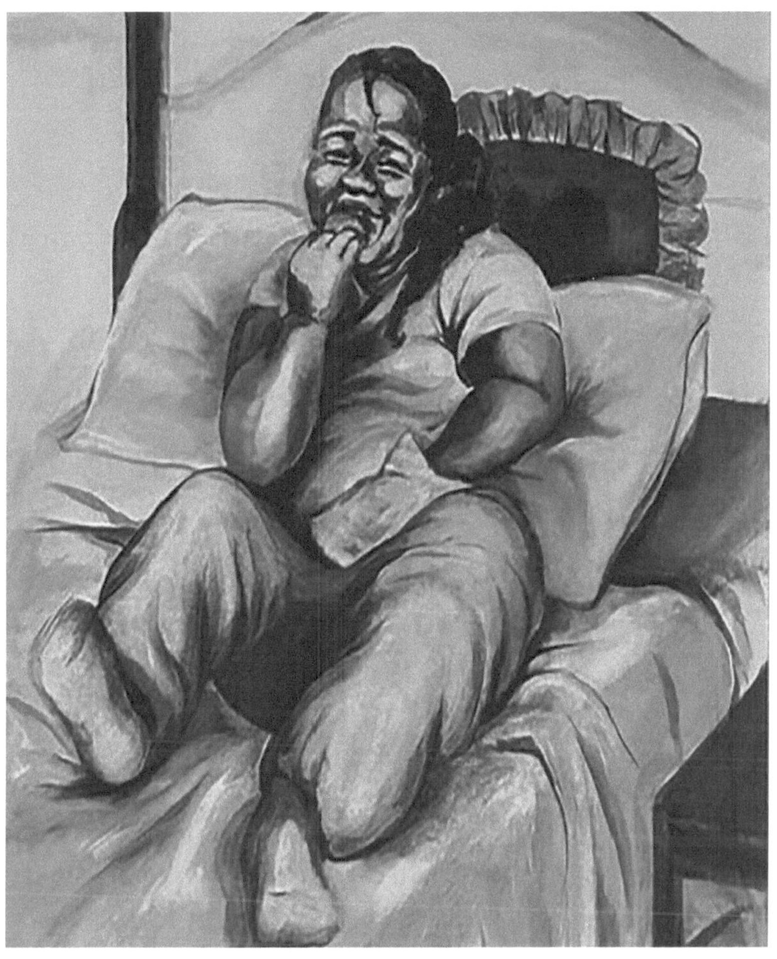

And finally, there was Sweetie Portly. Yes, you guessed it. She ate only the most sugary foods she could find: donuts, sugar-coated cereals, cupcakes, chocolates, pies, cookies, ice cream, tarts, gumballs, and of course, gallons and gallons of soda.

The Portly parents worked from home so they would not have to leave the house.

Craven took "online" courses so he wouldn't have to attend high school, and Sweetie just ate and watched TV all day long. As a result, they did not realize how big they were, or how slowly they moved, or how out of breath they were. In other words, they did not realize the sad condition they were in.

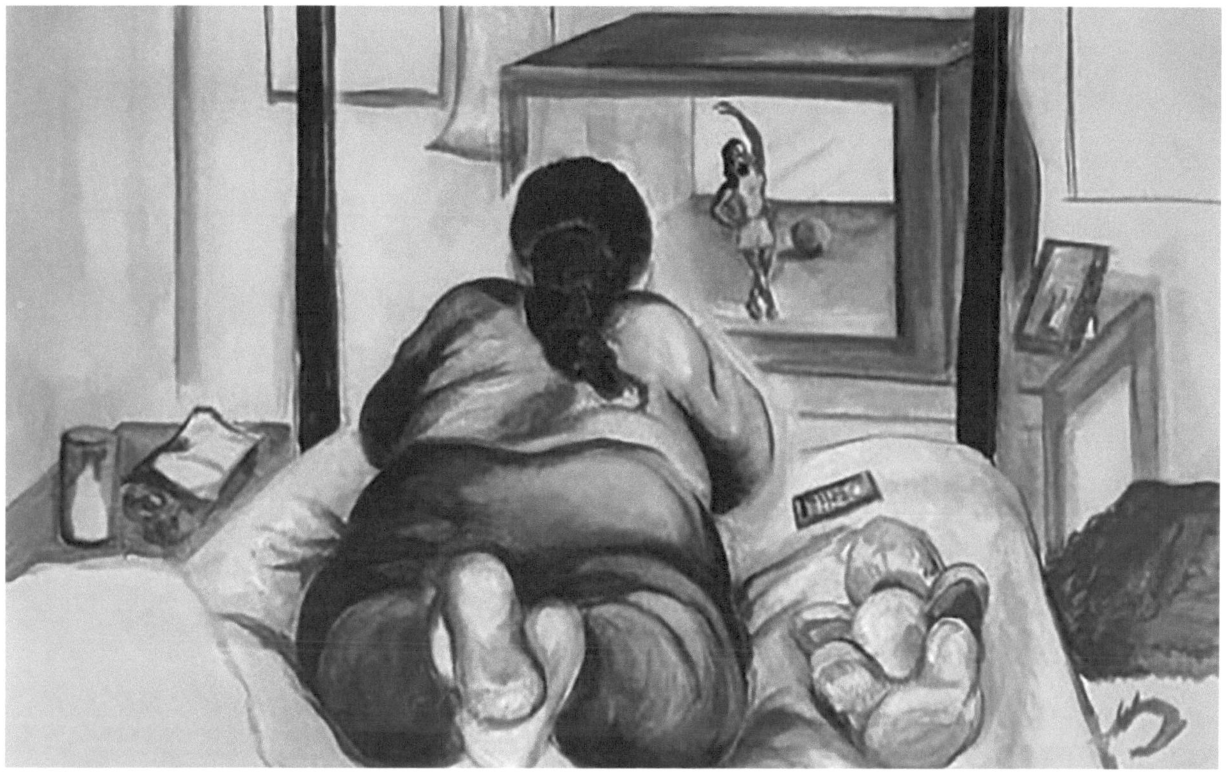

One day, while Sweetie was watching TV, a commercial for a new show suddenly appeared on the screen. In it was the most beautiful girl Sweetie had ever seen. The girl looked a lot like Sweetie but was much slimmer and had a lot more energy.

"Hey there, everyone, it's time for me. So let's get fit! I'm Elaine Energy," the girl's voice pulsated to the beat of the background music. Sweetie tried to push herself up in bed to get a better look at the TV.

Suddenly, Elaine Energy broke into the coolest dance Sweetie had ever seen. It looked simple enough, and the girl moved so smoothly to each beat of the music. After watching for a few minutes, Sweetie decided to try the dance, something called the "Swing, Sway, and Smile Slide."

Now, here's where the story gets interesting. Since the Portly family members rarely moved, it was a challenge for Sweetie to simply get off of her bed. Sweetie rolled to the right and lifted her legs over the edge of the bed. But to her dismay, she could not sit up. Why? Her large, portly stomach was in the way. So, she rolled the other way, and the next thing she knew... plop! Sweetie was flat on the floor. After a few struggling moments, Sweetie managed to claw her way to a standing position. She was so out of breath, she had to hold on to the post of her canopy bed to steady herself.

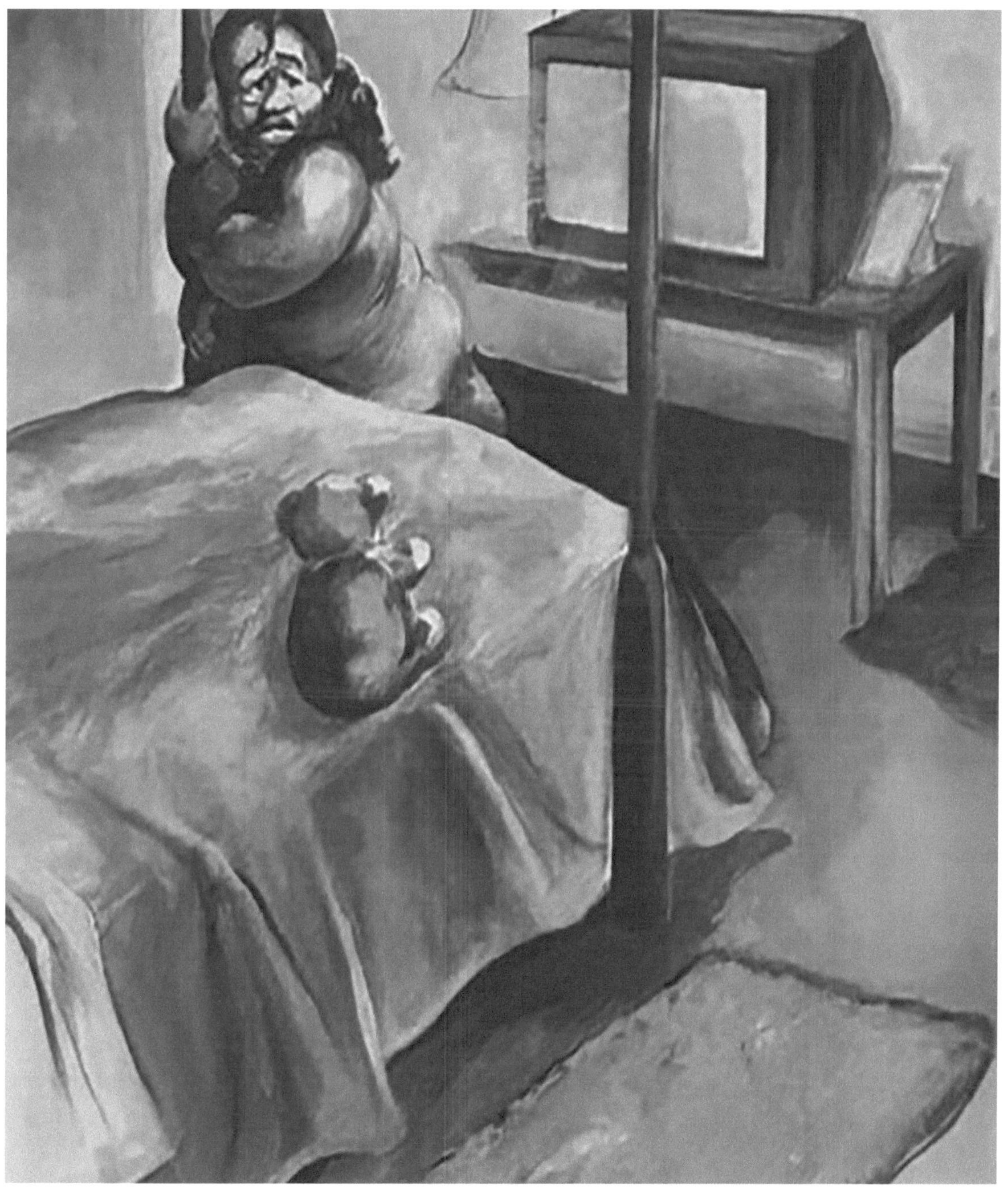

Once Sweetie was standing on her own two feet, she felt much better. As the music began to blast a steady rhythm, Sweetie tried to move. Two slide steps to the right, then two slide steps to the left. So far, so good! The next step was a turn. Sweetie had never turned her body all the way around, only to the right or to the left. But the pretty girl on the TV kept encouraging, "Come on, now, it's a three step turn. One, two, three and clap."

Sweetie tried to do the turn and fell backwards and landed on her bottom.

"Ouch!" she yelled. "Enough!"

Then Sweetie just sat in the middle of her floor and cried. As she sobbed with her head down, Elaine's voice from the TV whispered, "Swing, Sway, and Smile, so don't give up, change what you eat and change your luck."

The next day as Sweetie slugged along to the breakfast table, she thought about the voice on the commercial. "Change what you eat and change your luck." With that, instead of eating her usual three bowls of sugar-coated cereal with milk, she scoured the pantry and found a box of oatmeal. She quickly fixed a small bowl before the rest of the family arrived at the table.

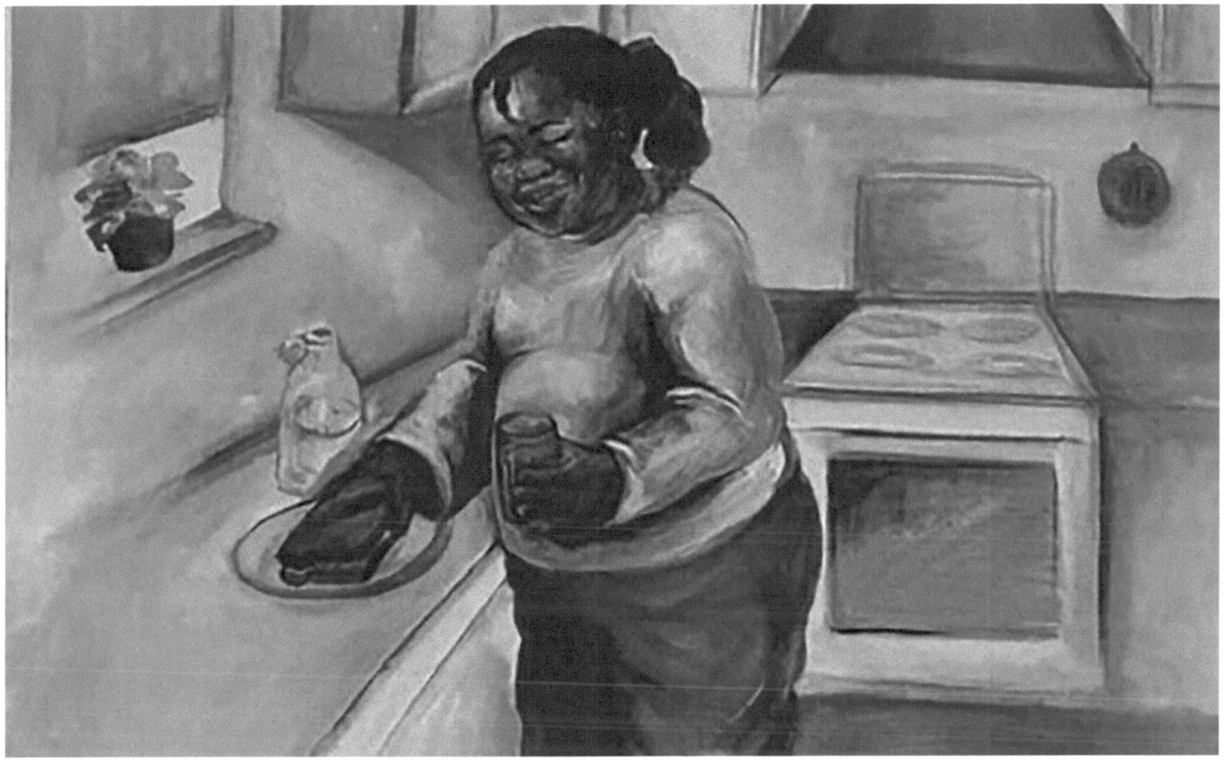

By the time her parents and her brother appeared, Sweetie was finished and washing her bowl.

When lunchtime rolled around, Sweetie again reached the kitchen before everyone else. Instead of her daily dose of donuts, cookies, and soda, she decided to make a tuna sandwich and drink a glass of apple juice. To her surprise, it was actually very tasty and filling, and she noticed that she felt much better.

Sweetie slugged her way back to her room and turned on her TV just in time to find one of her favorite shows. Once again, the same commercial appeared with the ever energetic Elaine Energy doing the "Swing, Sway, and

Smile Slide." This time, Sweetie was determined to do the dance all the way through. As the music pulsated from the screen, Sweetie began the dance - two slide steps to the right and two slide steps to the left, three steps, turn, and clap. To her surprise, Sweetie was able to do the turn. Awesome! She became so excited that she kept doing the dance over and over for at least an hour.

Sweetie couldn't wait until the next time to see the commercial with Elaine Energy. Like clockwork, Elaine appeared on Sweetie's TV, singing, dancing, and teaching Sweetie a few things about making healthy choices. This week, Elaine had a new dance to share. When Elaine started making some funny shapes with her body, Sweetie didn't quite get it. Then finally she listened to the Energy chant: "A, B, C, D, and E. All the vitamins your family needs!"

Wow! thought Sweetie, *That sounds* pretty cool. Not only did it sound cool, but Elaine had another cool dance for Sweetie to learn.

Sweetie had to form the shapes of each vitamin as quickly as it was rapped then step-hop and clap at the same time. She was supposed to do this four times in a row, alternating sides. Coordination was never a strong Portly family trait, but Sweetie was willing to try. She stepped on her foot twice, almost fell sideways three times, and couldn't get the clap until the twentieth time, but she never gave up. Finally, she was able to do the "Vitamin Shuffle." So what did all those letters mean? Elaine broke it down and rapped:

"A, B, C, D and E!

All the vitamins your family needs.

I said 'A' makes our eyes and teeth healthy and strong.

'B' we need for a fit heart all day long.

I said 'C' helps our body fight germs and disease. While 'D' gives us the tough bones to play with ease.

And last but not least, there's vitamin 'E'

That gives our skin the healthy glow that it needs.

A, B, C, D and E! All the vitamins your family needs."

For the next two weeks, Sweetie continued to make changes in her eating habits. She ate fewer and fewer sugary foods and did something no one else in her family had ever done. She began to drink water. Lots and lots of water. And then it happened. Her clothes started to become loose, and she had a lot more energy than she had ever had in the past. Everyday she did the "Swing, Sway, and Smile Slide" and the "Vitamin Shuffle" in her room to all kinds of music.

As her body began to change, her mood lifted, and she now wanted to leave the house and see what was on the other side of the front door. Her family started to notice the changes in Sweetie and was amazed at her transformation. Maybe there was something to eating healthier.

Sweetie convinced the rest of the family to abandon the fried, high-fat, junk food they had been accustomed to eating and to try the less-is-better approach. She also taught them how to do the "Swing, Sway, and Smile Slide" and the "Vitamin Shuffle." Soon, Mrs. Patricia Plump Portly and Craven Portly also started to notice changes of their own! Mr. O. Bese Portly even threw away the stinky green cigarettes so he could dance too.

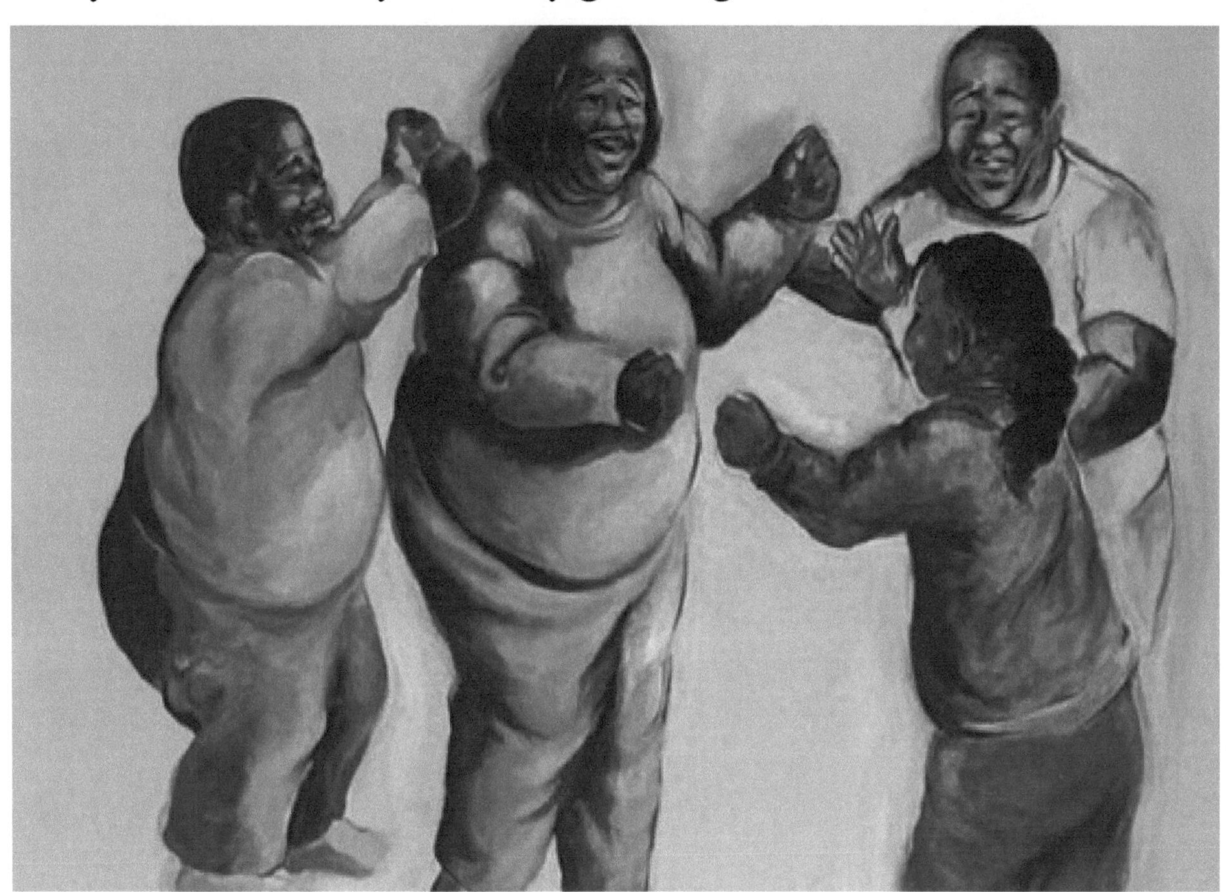

After some weeks later, a new Elaine Energy commercial appeared. This time, Elaine was just a little sad. This would be the final Elaine Energy commercial. Elaine looked Sweetie right in her eyes and said, "You've made wonderful progress since the time you first saw me, so now it's time to go outside and play!" And with that, the commercial clicked off and went straight to a program that was on the air.

Sweetie was ready to open the door and leave the house. Her family could not believe it. They gasped! No Portly had ever ventured beyond the inside of the blue polka dot house. Mrs. Portly actually liked the idea of leaving the house. Maybe now she could go to the market like the rest of her neighbors instead of having the groceries delivered. Craven liked the way he looked and was thinking about going to the local high school.

Mr. Portly began to think about working away from the house for the first time. So they gathered around a calendar and discussed a day for their "opening" of the door. Finally, after some haggling, they all agreed to the first Sunday of the next month.

So for the rest of the month, the Portly family continued to eat lots of fresh fruits and vegetables, whole grains, fish, and a little chicken or turkey every now and then. Mr. Portly found himself with a certain fondness for Mrs. Patricia's Turkey Burger Deluxe. There had not been a soda in the house for weeks as the beverage of choice was the pure, spring water from the Nimativ River that was delivered twice a month. The best part of their new lifestyle was the energetic dances led by Sweetie. Sweetie had become such an expert at the "Swing, Sway, and Smile Slide" and the "Vitamin Shuffle" that she started thinking about offering classes once she left the house.

The night before the first Sunday of the new month, the Portly family gathered to make sure they all wanted to take the next step. Unanimous!

They were on! Once that was settled, they rushed off to bed anxiously waiting for the "Opening."

The next morning, the sun rose majestically over the horizon and left a glaze of warmth across everything it touched. Sweetie was the first one up in the Portly house. She had selected an outfit to wear on this maiden voyage, and she wanted to surprise everyone. Craven prepared for his debut into the outside world by trimming some of his hair and actually combing it. This really must be a special occasion!

"Come on, everyone, it's time," called Mr. Portly to the rest of his family.

And like toy soldiers, they marched to the door and stood next to Mr. Portly.

And with one sweep of the arm, Mr. Portly opened the front door of the blue polka dot house on Twilight Lane. The new, improved, healthier Portly family emerged into the vast world. Now, they could do anything. Run, skip, hop, swim, play football, jump rope, dance, but most of all, live longer, happier lives.